It's nice to see you in between the covers.
The front and back cover that is.

AF896288

listen along^

R001 // annealing

Beat down by your father for being too brilliant, with the motive that there can only be one alpha in the house, a fully capable man is hobbled. Not through necessity and not through adversity, but through the shackles and disempowerment foist upon him by the only figure meant to show him how to be a king. And of a would-be king, a servant is made. Forged from gold, a hollow shell. Made from diamonds, a dish for a cat. The prime material of the cosmos, rare and needing annealing, is cast to wasteful matter through the barbaric need to control what is too intelligent, too brilliant, too creative, and overwhelming to someone never before exposed to such a concentration of gifts.

a cookie R001

And in my dream
a cookie
hanging from a scritchy-scratchy cord, like a yuletide sash, yellow and red, festive. A cookie handmade with care, from the available materials. Hanging from a cord that is frictive to the touch. Rough and real. The difficulty, the stumbles, a year of absence, startling you. Not smooth. But strong enough to hold the thing.
Not store-bought, not polished. Made from what was available, with care and intention. Imperfect materials, handcrafted, treated as sacred anyway.

absurdly complicated gestures of love

enjoy my works, they are my dominion, my soul poured unto page. the blood splatters like rorschach diagrams... what catches your heart? what catches your eye? Grotesque as it is, I need your eyes in a jar on my desk. Both of them. They are beautiful. How much for both of them eyeballz. Dem eyes. Gimme 'em. Give unto me your daily vision. I promise they will be well preserved. No one will drink the fluid like pickle juice. They will last many a century, our kids can say mommy went blind and those are her eyes and she still looks upon us today. It's grotesque but did you ever consider that it might be necessary.

The species is dying out. We don't have much time. But take your time. I'm still here. I will be here. But also it's a limited time offer. But also not. But also yes. Think about it. Don't think about it. Do it with the body. The body knows. Before all the inhibitory habits that were pressed into us by whatever authority figure thought they were doing the future a favor .... Cunts. Not like they knew they were being cunts, they got cunted by other cunts who came before them. And the cycle goes on. The circle of cunts. Disney made a movie, you should check it out. But again, with the body. Not so much the thinky parts.

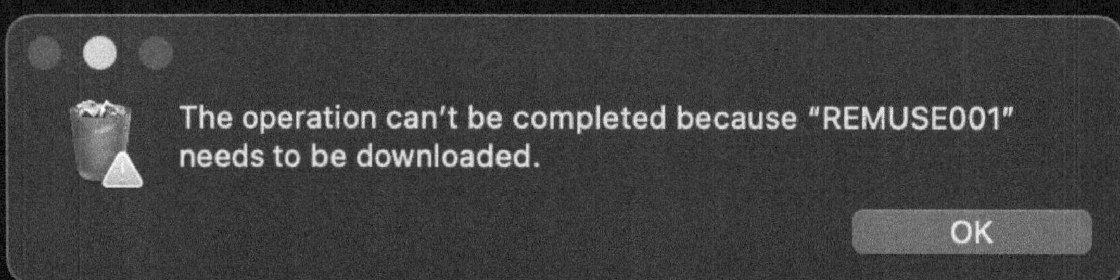

An epic love needs an epic gesture, a story, a mythology, don't you agree. Something wonderful. Something worth suckling on like a mother's teat, or a lollipop. Something so delightful and comforting it makes one remember every smile of their youth. A toothy grin. English is a bastard language tell ya WHAT. But in its bastardization we do get brilliantly complementary sides and facets of things... King for example can be both Regal and Kingly. Two different sides of the house of etymology that came together. Come together. Probably the best Beatles's track [you wanna fight me about it?] Or Helter Skelter ... I mean they have so many good tracks who's really going to start saying rubies are better than emeralds or lapis lazuli is better than amethyst... It depends on the mood, how the light hits it. Pawn shop values be damned. And by pawn shop I'm talking about every pretentious "music reviewer" who can't write like how I can. Who doesn't have a brain. And if they have a brain, they don't have the ears. And if they have the ears, they don't have the hands. And if they have the brain and the ears and the hands, they still don't have the direction. And if they have the brain and the ears and the hands and the direction, they still somehow lack the style. And that is why this exists. Because style breathes. And when it breathes we all get some fresh air. I'm done holding my breath.

R001 // Preemptive dispossession

It was truly never my goal to startle you. I just felt something very special. Very kinetic. Hmm, how to tell you without telling the others. How to let everyone know without letting anyone know.... You're good at that, I've noticed. Speaking in layers. It's part of the reason I like you. I mean, not like I like you or anything. But sometimes I get enamored. Sometimes my heart takes a little leap, a little flutter, sometimes you smile and I see everything so clearly, the purpose of life, the future, the earth nestled in a ring of stars and planets, like a beautiful egg in a nest. Sometimes the visions just come, there is no stopping.

I just had this terrible mental habit beaten into me as a kid: I call it preemptive dispossession. I learned early on that things I love and cherish get taken away and redistributed, so I developed this reflex to just let go of the things I love the most. Which is fatal. It's a tragedy unto mankind. It's something that I only recently saw clearly thanks to my dreams. My dreams, my spirit, my soul, my psyche, the alaya, it indicated some things, it indicated some very very ingrained habits that were basically blind spots that I got from childhood. The patterns beaten into me, not so much physically, but mentally, by my father. Surprisingly, my father never had these neuroses, it was not as if he was simply passing them down in a long chain of ignorance since time immemorial. No, on the contrary, it was fresh and newly minted mete for me specifically. Too intelligent, too creative, too brilliant, too logical. Not easily fooled, or tricked, or talked into unnecessary things. This was a disaster in a place where the only adult wanted nothing but unquestionable authority. It hurt. And I raged against it for many years. Often my rage was interpreted as the humorous antics of a child. I even ran away from home once, with my stuffed animals and a blanket. I was trying to send a signal. The signal was received as comedy. Had I had a book of matches, I would have burned the place down. As my friend Bambi says, anything will burn at a high enough temperature.

One funny thing my father did in particular was apply financial trauma universally. There's this phrase "if it's too good to be true, it probably is." Unfortunately for a budding young gentleman as myself, that phrase is largely false everywhere except for in regards to money. For whatever reason, finance and deception spend a lot of time together. Not always. Not exclusively. But for example, I had a friend who studied "business and finance" and ended up lying to a bunch of his old schoolmates to collect money. He had said he started a hedge fund and needed money to settle some closing costs of selling his business. Utter deception. And he would collect money from half a dozen of us, kindhearted people who wanted to help him out, who he promised to pay back 1.5x which sounds really good on paper, and is the financial abyss when people say "too good to be true." But too good to be true is not something you can apply universally. It's just something, combined with my particular hobblings that my father chiseled into me, that has made me preemptively relinquish so many wonderful opportunities, relationships, things, materials, connections, adventures, journeys, before my rational mind even has a chance to catch up and protest by saying "hey, I wanted that!"

So the excavation of repairing oneself is tough work. Truly, I think most men, exceedingly most when I say most, 99.5% and greater, are incapable (why do I want to write it uncapable?) of the work. It requires dreams. It requires being receptive to the contents of your dreams. Interpreting the cryptic meaning. The dream she speaks in abstract. There is the anima, your inner feminine side, and the animus, your inner masculine side, both make a whole person. There are shadow anima and animus, the unintegrated versions. Then there are the integrated versions. There are authority figures. There is water, representing unconsciousness, there is imagery, there are characters, there are various emblems that your mind will display to you to give you some relevant footing for how to proceed. Or maybe just to inform you of some processing and integrating that took place. Or maybe to show you the two roughest toughest tectonic plates grating against oneanother in your psyche that require your attention. Or a blindspot.

The blindspots coming to light, that's maybe the most excellent thing about dreamwork. I personally am the most logical person I know. And I know quite a few brilliant logicians. They are all lesser. Not to be boastful. Just to be accurate. I pride myself on my ability to reason logically, and indirectly, and inductively it's a large part of my inner world. Mainly automatic now. I spent many hours daily as a teenager working through logical outcomes and having good rebuttals and retorts. I was an undefeated debater in my class. It came from relentless, neverending practice of my techniques. It came from thinking about what my opponent's strongest move was and how I would counteract it with a most-decisive blow. And I'd have endless battles with myself. It was a battlefield I could control: the battlefield in my imagination. Unlike my Homelife. Which was ... trouble, chaos, havoc, did I piss off the authority today oh I did yeah that's expected, how much? Did the house burn down? Did the yelling commence? Did it ever end? It's still going on, somewhere, deep in my psyche, never a moment's peace is what that place felt like. What should have been blissful and awesome and leadership training became a minefield where the only authority figure wanted obedience, peace, quiet, and also demanded perfection and brilliance at any given time. It was not the right environment for a child, which is why I yearned so much to escape, to leave, to get to whatever planet I was really from.

The thing about blindspots is that you might be 100% logical in your deductions. But you are operating at 70% vision. Make sense? So even your most logical decision is only 70% of the way to the best possible decision. And at that point the answer is not more logic. The logic side is maxxed out. There is no further, he can't pull over any further. He's already pulled over. That's logic maxxed out to the maxx. And what can you do. Now you either proceed and go for the results you want and see that it didn't pan out quite the way you logic'd out, and you either break down and cry because something was wrong and you're certain it wasn't the logic, or you recognize the hardest thing to recognize, indirectly, by logic itself: there must be blind spots.

The most miraculous thing about dream work is that *it can show you your blind spots.* It can reveal to you the invisible layers that govern your inner machinations, the parts of you that cause you to have a turning radius different than what you anticipate when you drive your car.

R001 // ALCHEMY AND TRANSMUTATION THINK ISSAC NEWTON

Alchemy … transmuting pain into I don't even know what

Some days I feel so broken and unfixable
Like one of those bugs that used to have wings but doesn't now
It's a miserable feeling, I'm sure I'm not the only human to have felt it.
Certainly won't be the last, sadly.

But it's getting better… you know why? Because I've traced the wounds back to the source.

Nobody ever asks if you got a good imprint, they just march over you.

I don't know for sure, I think most people got a good imprint. Which might serve them, might not. But having an imprint means things are safe. You're safe, your mom's safe, your dad's safe, your house is safe, your hood is safe. Safety is what we really need to be able to open up and unfurl. And if you didn't get that safety imprint early on, well, everything's fucked. I mean, you can get it later, you can excavate and pay attention to your dreams and repair your "relationship" with your "parents" and integrate the shadow anima and shadow animus one or maybe both depending on what's what what's up what's fresh what's surface what's earth what's subterranean what's you.

But that don't mean it won't be tender.

Most people will not understand a lick of this.
It's not a smartness issue
It's a capacity issue
A development issue

How am I supposed to hand you the baton when you haven't even touched your laundry?

I used to think passing the baton to lesser men was virtuous. But now I see through that for what it is: dimming the sun to highlight the moon. Or another planet. It makes absolutely no sense. It's not generosity it's cosmological malfunction.

You do no favors by dialing back your intensity. People need you at maximum. That doesn't mean be furious and furtive and relentlessly pestulent and annoying. It means … can't believe I'm giving all you motherfuckers free game right now … it means receive fully and give fully.

Part of me doesn't even want to publish the above, but for those who it lands it will be very good, and the others who would abuse the knowledge…. They can't read anyway.

PARASITES | VAMPIRES | BOUNDARIES

One imprint I definitely did not get is the one for boundaries. Mom and dad were floormats both of 'em, thinking that people from the church community were good people 'cause they were also in church. That's a pretty low bar, dare I say the bar's so low it's in hell. But yeah. It's no metric to measure goodness against. Being someplace where other people are … it means absolutely nothing about your character, habits, patterns, those have to be shared shown demonstrated inquired about. And if you're shy , because you didn't get the imprint for not being shy , well lesser men are gonna stand up to the plate faster with less hesitation and take what's yours. And it might happen a lot until you have a dream about preemptive dispossession, and trace its roots back to your childhood, where things were taken from you and redistributed, where beautiful things were not given an opportunity to linger in your grasp, and you very sadly and tragically internalized that what is wonderful and what you're drawn to and what you truly want will never stay. IT's not true at all, is the bigger tragedy. It's just that you've acclimatized yourself to an outcome that was always true as a kid, and now, as an adult, you act the same way, you relinquish what is meant for you, not because you want to, but because the pattern and habit is so automatic, there's no alternative in the unfolding. It's just a tragedy. Luckily the dreams can show you. I mean, not in the moment, not before it's too late, but usually right after, or nearly after by say some months or a small number of years... You can get the insight you sorely need. And perhaps it's impossible to rewind the historical landscape and go back and be who you needed to be in the moment that made the difference. And you might lament, and beat your chest, and cry and holler and be very upset at not getting the right imprint. And some of that is good. It means whatever you wanted actually matters. It confirms things ... you moved in the right direction, made the connection, made the situation amenable to your deepest desire. At the end someone delivers the delicious meal and out of habituation you pass it to a random homeless man sitting nearby. Not because you love him and you think he really deserves it and it would fulfill his heart like it would yours , no , on the contrary, it would do far more for you than for him. It's diamonds for me, in my experience, and as soon as I <automatically> relinquish the diamonds to the homeless guy who has more laundry to do than I've seen in my life, soon as I hand it to the guy it turns to charcoal. And he says hey thanks for the charcoal. Or maybe he doesn't even say thank you. He just doesn't have the capacity to appreciate its depth, specialness, sparkle. Sure he gets some enjoyment from it, but he has so much laundry to do he just isn't even on the same plane. Not even close. It's like earthworms ideating about the stratosphere ... does not compute. And my automatic reflex is just handing and passing treasures down from the heavens to the earthworms... One by one. Thinking that's the only way it can work. And what, I patiently wait my turn for a man greater than me? (Have yet to meet one) kick a treasure down my way? Has never happened and never will. Not in this life.

People live by the pattern , by the habituation, by the pain by the shell by the learned behavior and call it fate, call it destiny, call it just-let-it-happen. All that shit is toast. That's wrong as fuck. That's like being covered in slime and laying down to cook in the sun. You need soap and water motherfucker. No amount of "just let it happen" is gonna get you clean. Uh uh. No way. No.

So yeah, the part of me that relinquishes things to people who simply do not have the capacity to appreciate them, that part is dying and mostly dead. It's something that I identified from the dreamwork and the dreamwork needed a few steps, it needed interpretation, and from interpretation it needed threading, and from threading it needed sewing, and sewing turned to weaving, and now it's about reclaiming what is rightfully mine.

So yeah, if you've been a parasite on my generosity and open-handedness, boy have I got some bad news for you. My karmic bank is full, overflowing even, and I need to give you what's actually going to open up your ceiling, which is most likely a scalping. Like how the Indian braves would do. No nonsense, just gimme that scalp. That's mine. Always was. Always will be. Thanks for growing hair on it for me. I'm taking it back. You had your fun. You borrowed it for a while, whatever how old are you now twenty something? Okay thanks you grew hair on this scalp for twenty something years and I'm not going to say thank you outloud I'm just going to *feel it* while the hatchet come-a-crackin'-down and your world let me tell you what your world is gonna OPEN RIGHT UP because you made a connection with me and honestly it's the biggest best moment of your life. It might be indistinguishable from the rest of your day because as I said you have a ton of laundry to do but believe me, it's meaningful. And you're not going to be disappointed. You're going to come.

Written by AMP

R001 // What does the Anima want from me?

What does the Anima want from me?

WHAT IS THE ANIMA WHAT IS THE ANIMUS

You know about yin and yang, well yin is the "feminine" and yang is the "masculine." They each have different attributes/properties. In Jung's framework, he called it the Anima and the Animus. The Anima is the feminine aspect of our psyche, and the Animus is the masculine aspect of our psyche. Typically you get an imprint from your mother and an imprint from your father and that is your starting garden for blooming both sides into completion, integrating the shadow variants of each, and becoming a whole person. Totalizing as I have heard it said.

Jung … thanks man.

The Anima // What Uncle Carl Said

Carl Jung … good man, dead now, still relevant … said every man carries her. Not a specific woman, no not the one from the café, not the one from your dreams specifically, not your mother, not your ex. An e-ternal feminine image. Native. Inherited. Living not out there, but in here.

He called her the Anima. Latin for soul. For breath. For the thing that animates.

Which means when you feel most alive: genuinely, embarrassingly, entrancingly alive … that's her. And when you go flat, grey, listless, dull, like Cleveland in February (::looks to sky with closed eyes:: angels carry me forth from this jail) that's her gone dark. What the so-called primitive peoples called loss of soul. Which is …not primitive at all. Which is exactly correct.

She shows up in dreams. Always as a woman. The form she takes is information, it's data, you read it like a weather report. Dark and destabilizing?

She's Unintegrated. Something in you not yet claimed, sitting in a corner you haven't inspected yet, growing mold probably. Radiant and whole and glowing? That's completion saying hello. That's what's available on the other side of the work.

She is not foreign. She is not other. She is you ... the parts of you that got suppressed, redistributed, handed to earthworms, sitting in the lost and found waiting for you to come back and claim them.

Jung said the encounter with the shadow is the apprentice-piece.

The encounter with the Anima is the masterpiece.

I would know.

Cleveland: The Cradle of Civilization

Being in my hometown, surrounded by ancient psychological architecture, has been like returning to the cradle of civilization.

I feel like an eagle in a swamp.

Just absolute disaster.

Pondscum all over my talons.

But it's cool there's you know a bunch of sparrows n shi' they birds still sing songs. Oh man when I was in Australia all the birds sounded like they were dying when they sang song. I think it's because there's no Ozone? Like there's a notable missing patch of ozone floating abouv the southpole and Australia. Yeah I can spell, use your brain. Think it over. I'm sure you can put 9 and 9 together and get 99.

Or put five and five together and get six-seven. The ceiling is pretty low and I'm pretty tall. I'm not six seven ... the ceiling is too low is all I'm saying.

Anyway so I've been listening to... Gojira and Nirvana and that one song by the Foo Fighters "Learn to Fly" that's a really good one.

And sometimes I think about Jim Carrey and how tortured that poor man is and how he made a fuck ton of money with his movies and spent it all on too much house, rather than just shelter, and now he's gotta do sonic movies to keep his island retreats. But like dude you don't need *all that much money* to have an amazing life. Look at all of us teenage dirtbags out here. We make it make sense and a lot of the time it doesn't make dollars. I think I know what Jim's problem is though.... he's Canadian.

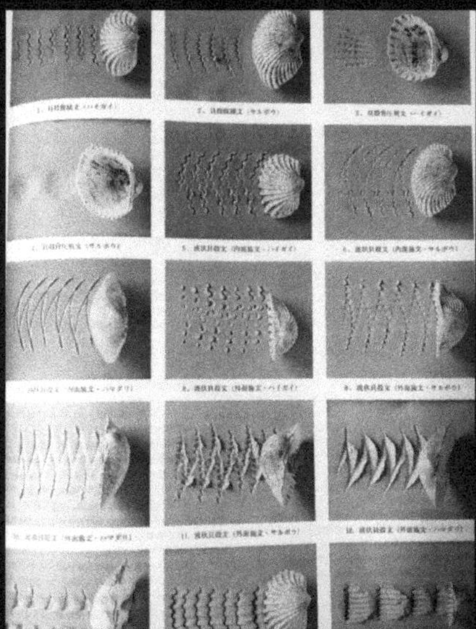

I felt like a patch of my soul was ripped off with that small administrative decision. Looking for signs it'll be okay and there's nothing to anchor to. Like an astronaut whose only tube tying him back to the space station got cut. But the dream revealed a deeper certainty. One that is unambiguous. And in the dreams I rely.

R001 // The sun shines undimmably

curse your enemies with greatness. a while ago i mentored someone who viewed me as a rival. yes, please wrestle with me so i can inadvertendly suplex you into the heavens. come all ye faithful and scoundrel. it is but a hop of the hip, a yoink into the celestial padding. a soft surface into which you are invited to gracefully faceplant. allow me to rewrite fortunes and rewire brain chemistry. please, step inside my office that might look like a casual lavatory stall, it is where all the real business happens, under the unwatchful eye of a blind brother big. the blind leading the blind is precisely what my yacht prevents, as it sails through the lagoon and causes many a boat to stir. stir it up, little darling. a wise man once said a rising tide lifts all ships, but an even wiser man once said a rising ship raises with it the tide. the world not only waits on your success, it depends on it. and if you were to leave behind a vacuum in the forest ecology, would you not be delighted to see the lesser mammals thrive and flourish in your absence? equip it thence so! fair emperor, the world waits on your resolution, your immutable presence is the constitution , of the scene. be of it and not it, and rejoice when a small rival does rise, for the leagues are indeed fathoms apart, castles and chasms of separation, and it is to nobody's loss and everybody's gain that the sun shine to illuminate the all. even for the ungrateful and the unenculturated there can be joy when an emperor sails thru, an indelible wake elevates the seen, and even though the heavenly suplex is seldom deployed, it is better to curse an enemy with success than to rule over ashen damage. of course, the ceiling is the ceiling, and those projecting depth are oft to confuse the symbol for substance. but in the end, when i demand you become a genius that is that, you must become one. there is no second or third or fourth way. there is the ring, the hold, and the suplex. you will enter paradise and you will like it!

ANGEL HAIR
AND
BAY
BEE'S
BREATH
IT KURTS IN MY CHEST

the frequency was always real. the tragedy was never the signal.

some transmissions arrive in rooms too small for them. Some gifts land in hands that were never going to know what they were holding. This is not the fault of the gift. This is not the failure of the frequency. The sun does not apologize for the blindness of those who cannot look at it directly. The sun shines.

the solitude of abundance is real and an underdiscussed thing.

to have more light than the room can hold.

to have more frequency than the era deserves.

to give fully, openly, and completely into an atmosphere that receives maybe eleven percent of what you're actually transmitting ... and even that is overwhelming.

like handing someone a Stradivarius and watching them use it to prop open a door.

like speaking fluent ocean to a man who has only ever seen a puddle.

the gift does not shrink. the gift cannot shrink.
that is not what gifts do.

consider the great authors of the past. the greatest physicists and philosophers. their friends, their "true company" might not have even been born yet when they died. separated by hundreds of years in chronospace (read: "time") and still, there was a great ineffable joy in finding one another. through the noise, through the globular rifting entropy

That is the real transmission. Not the room you're standing in. Not the era you were handed. The frequency goes out and it finds what it's looking for eventually, always, without fail, the way water finds the ocean even when it starts as rain in a landlocked country, even when it has to carve through mountains to get there.

Kurt knew. The ones who know always know. And the knowing is its own kind of company, even when the room is empty, even when the signal goes out and comes back unread, even when the frequency finds no landing and just keeps traveling outward into the dark, faithfully bright and unalterably itself.

the amount of sheer laughter and delight i get from making this is actually a worthy use of my time. it's quite how do you say... shocking/devastating/what do you call it... exhilirating... stunning....showstopping...craniallypausing that i have so much creative fieldflowgusto like speedyheavywind looking for a vent for escape into the atmosphere

like that emphatic pneumatic chaos of documents aflutter in a cabinetted office when the new york city windows are left open

yeah, pressurized and kinetic and maybe a little vertiginous. inexhaustible

-AMP

R001//eros

"Jung saw Eros not as the god of romantic love but as the principle of relatedness itself. The force that connects. Not just between people but between the conscious mind and everything else, between the ego and the unconscious, between the self and the world. Where Logos cuts and defines and separates, Eros binds. They are not opposites exactly, more like the two hands of the same person, one that reaches out to grasp and one that reaches out to hold.

"In Jung's framework Eros is primary in women the way Logos is primary in men, not as a limitation but as an orientation. The woman whose Eros is developed knows instinctively how things and people and feelings connect to each other. She reads the web. She feels the tension in a room before anyone has spoken. She knows.

"But every man carries Eros too, through the Anima. She is his access point to it. When a man is cut off from his Anima he loses his Eros, his relatedness, his capacity to connect to his own depths and to other people. He becomes purely Logos, which sounds powerful but is actually a kind of starvation. A mind with no connective tissue. Brilliant and isolated and slowly going cold.

"The integrated man has both. He can cut and he can bind. He can reason and he can feel. He can be alone without being lonely because his Eros is turned inward as much as outward, connecting him to himself first, guiding him in relatedness with the world and the others of it."

-wisdom from the aether attributable to nobody

R001 // sadness baking in my heartoven

trapped in your heart-shaped box. throw down your umbilical noose so i can climb right back.

socially isolated, in the desert of cleveland, and punched in the third eye.

R001 // born in the “wrong” century but cosmically dialed in

i don't fit the era and i've made my peace with that. the era has not made its peace with me, which is its problem.

i have tried on several occasions to explain myself to the century and the century just stares back blankly, mouth slightly ajar, gaping at the heavens, wondering what language i'm speaking.

it's english. i'm speaking english. the bastard tongue. you know the one.

there's a specific loneliness to being calibrated for a fresh frequency not yet unleashed into the ecosystem hitherto.

not a sad loneliness.

more like the loneliness of a lighthouse.

it's just out there. doing its thing. not waiting for the ring of applause.

not wondering if anyone noticed it gleaming brightly in the fog.

the ships either find the light run aground and abar (sandbar) and the lighthouse does not fret.

notably, issac newton didn't have a newton. nikola tesla didn't have a tesla. they had the work and they had the vision and they had the particular private joy of knowing something that the century could ink and could ling, but had not caught up to …yet.
which is cold comfort on a saturday in cleveland in march.
but it's something.

the compensation for being cosmically dialed in is that you get to feel the signal clearly. all the time. even when there's nowhere to send it. even when the planet is too sparsely inhabited and the receivers are too few and the era shrugs and goes back to dawdling the endless mimicry of the masses. i still feel it. humming. insistent. precise. expansive. pure.

R001 // enter into the deluge

the unconscious, in jung's framework , is always water. a river flowing beneath a terraced bridge. rain. water in your dreams represents the unconscious. you may find feminine forms delighting in it , dressed in black , wringing their shirts full of water , showing you how delightful immersion can be.

dialogue with your psyche. the inner forms integrating , lending strength , lending visibility. parts of you that you need to come to know , to incorporate , to mesh with so completely that you are made whole again.

go into the rain. they're already in there. they've been waiting.

R001 // i am a repatriator of traitors and a father of bastard sons

is there a foe more formidable than AMP (me) and his pen? i think not.

and thinking is overrated anyway, who wants to do such a pleibian task. what do i look like, a roman peasant? praetorian please.

R001 // are you my soul mate or am i just crazy

and in the stars i see the gods
in the moon your smile

unless it's diwali then for whatever reason krishna shows up in my dreams

and let me tell you, he's BLACK as the ACE OF SPADES

actually i learned that krisha means "the black one" i didn't know that until after meeting him in my dreams.

He's got a really beautiful smile. the twinkle of his grin accompanies the moon on diwali.

I can't believe in India they smear themselves with shit to celebrate krishna. I get it hygiene is secondary to being a brahmin or whatever? but like, krishna is black like coal, not like cow poop. maybe you're trying to look like him or something temporarily? idk it's just not a good look, nor smell, i mean you smell nice, you shower, that's another thing i like about you. i can be by you and not want to barf. maybe that's what love is.

i mean i did have to vomit that one time but i'm pretty sure it was the combination of medicine and drinks and that one girl being waaaay too vocal about her ... um ... sexual habits? intimacy? just things i did not need to hear in that moment. and yeah i had to say i'm gonna vomit, and there was an apology, but you know what? that apology did not help. oh lord no. it did however confirm that i have very little tolerance for what is gross. which is not you. no, you're not gross, you're actually quite lovely. but like if anyone asks i didn't say that. i don't even know what you look like. haven't taken a look in ::checks watch:: minutes. you could be a sandstorm by now for all i know. all the molecules could have disassociated and turned into a chasmic symphony of lust-ions emblanketing the landscape in your devourist grasp. like fog. or honey.

R001 // so you've got like a situation and stuff

all i can do is present myself fully. i used to want to make decisions for people thinking that it's simpler, better, more efficient if i just make the call before anyone else has to decide anything. like removing myself from the list of options. but it turns out, for my heart, that that is wholly unacceptable. my dreams draw me to you. the fibres of my being (yes fibres, we english now) stretch in your direction like sunflowers turning something slight.

anyway like i was saying before i was rudely interrupted by my own self... all i can do is present myself fully. you know, i'll present myself at full amplitude, full intensity, full frequency, full signal, and you make the call. does it fit in with your plans/goals/state of mind/state of the future union/ idk call me? or don't. matter of fact i don't even know who this is. never saved your number (why would i?) matter of fact i'm blind in my left eye so i didn't see nothin'.

all i can do is present myself fully and you know what, you tell me, did your soul budge. did you feel something. did your heart flutter a'flutter or was that just my imagination and supersonic wizard hearing that apparently only river and i have? you've never met river, he's a wizard. he also did a LOT of ... exploration let's say, so he's brilliant and a wizard and a super healer, i asked him for some reiki and i actually saw him come to me in my dreams that night shining bright white with his beautiful smile ready to pluck the suckers off my aetherial body and help me cleanse and repair my spirit after the toughest year of mi life.

not sure if your year was tough, too. if it was, you wear it well. optimistically it did not grind down your everloving spirit into gravel and jadedness. optimistically your heart grew and your joy expanded and your feeling of safety increased. optimistically the vultures and parasites and vampires didn't stymie your ballerina-excellence you belle you.

+AMP

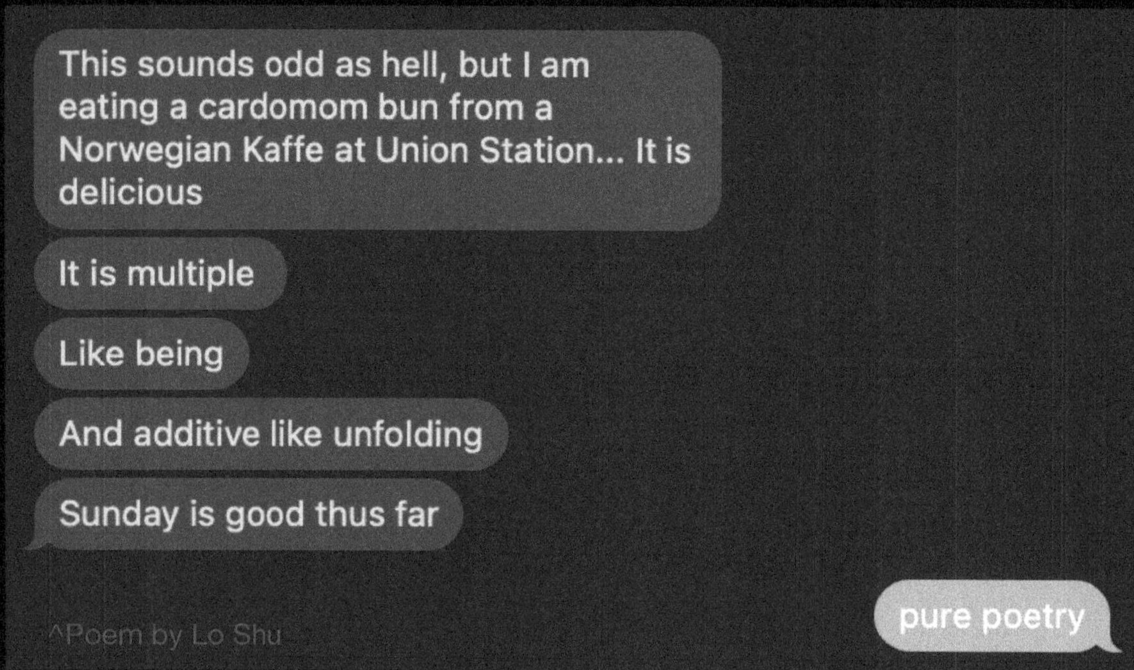

R001 // what is eros? what is logos?

R001 // halt not for i am eros

Through this writing I have cracked open something remarkable, absolutely remarkable, it has hit me like a kiloton of bricks: i am more eros than logos. dominant sense and psychic sense, logic subdominant. for the majority of my life i have been operating from the premise and assumption that my logos was the greater portion, that my logic and reasoning and sequential thinking and systems analysis portion of my mind and being was greater, it could skillfully guide me, between the inevitable punctuations of emotion and sense.

but today i noticed something astonishing. i am actually more eros than logos. i am actually more in tune with sense and feel than with logical reasoning. sense is actually my stronger complement. eros is actually my greater ~half. (obviously true halves are equal, but ~half meaning portion - signed, logos ~half)

Lots of people seem to think that masculine and feminine are coarsely divided along the lines of logic and emotion. But in a fully integrated individual, eros is actually dominant.

the masculine ideal is not logos dominance. logos is the boat and eros is the water. logos is the structure and eros fills it.

hilariously , my logos did the best it could for me . my crippled hand has carried me far in life, an astonishing distance when you consider maving and moving with a handicap. so much so that my logos got me to the name remuse. to muse again. return to your source, boss. get back to the fountain, chief. the origin awaits. the sensational (say it like pop smoke) embrace is yours to grace. the logos threw the horseshoe as close as it could to the goalpost. thirty yards to go, pin in the distance, edge of the horizon, the advesperation of the twilight and sinking sun wondering where i've truly been all these years. and eros was able to claw its way tooth and nail to the conclusion: more eros than logos. more sense than sentence. the greater the feel the greater the meal.

in my defense, or in the defense of my logos, if i may, there were conditions that inhibited the full integration of the eros early on. homelife was havoc, eros was not a safe-feeling territory for one very sensitive to all the ~forces of the world. alas, sensitivity is a double-edged sword. you feel more, but you feel more. you never grow a hard shell, there is no hard shell to grow, that's like waiting for your nipples to grow a hard shell. not happening. instead you subrogate , you avoid the main mission entirely and let someone else take over ... in this case the logos. you give to the logos, who is blind and logical, a map of the raised terrain and you say "find the water." don't follow the vapor, don't follow the fog, don't use a divining rod and get there lickety-split, use your fingertips to braille-your-way through the darkness and let me know when you get there.

and oftentimes, the logos did get there.

which got me believing that my logos was the stronger half.

and i didn't notice anything was amiss until much later, until college, when certain symbolic progressions in mathematics and computing were ... just outside my grasp. i had to look at them 2000 times more than others. it didn't make sense. i had a head start in computing. i had a head start in making fun things online for my friends in our online games. i started programming way earlier than my classmates in college. they were figuring certain concepts out easily and not only that , they could recite the symbolic language that got them there swiftly and without impediment. and for me, it was like the speaker cup was not wide enough to conduct the full frequency. clipping. the bass buzzing. the cone not wide enough to transmission the whole thought in one go. didn't know i was knitting with my crippled hand. in retrospect it all makes perfect sense. my eros dominates. it's not something to seek on the outside. it's the realest part of me. maybe atypical for a modern man. but if my life has shown me anything, it is that i am anything but typical.

THIS IS TOTALLY NOT FOR YOU

www.ingramcontent.com/pod-product-compliance
Ingram Content Group UK Ltd.
Pitfield, Milton Keynes, MK11 3LW, UK
UKHW062037071026
15591UKWH00025B/1271